THE LITTLE BOOK OF
Circle
Processes

A New/Old Approach
to Peacemaking

KAY PRANIS

Good Books

Intercourse, PA 17534
800/762-7171
www.GoodBooks.com

Cover photograph by Howard Zehr.

Design by Dawn J. Ranck
THE LITTLE BOOK OF CIRCLE PROCESSES
Copyright © 2005 by Good Books, Intercourse, PA 17534
International Standard Book Number: 978-1-56148-461-4
Library of Congress Catalog Card Number: 2005015575

Library of Congress Cataloging-in-Publication Data
Pranis, Kay.
  The little book of circle processes : a new/old approach to peacemaking
/ Kay Pranis.
    p. cm.
  Includes bibliographical references.
  ISBN 1-56148-461-X (pbk.)
  1. Conflict management. 2. Healing circles. I. Title.
HM1126.P73 2005
303.6'9--dc22   2005015575

Table of Contents

1.
Introduction

"We're all lovers and we're all destroyers. We're all fright-ened and at the same time we all want terribly to trust. This is part of our struggle. We have to help what is most beautiful to emerge in us and to divert the powers of darkness and vio-lence. I learn to be able to say, 'This is my fragility. I must learn about it and use it in a constructive way.'"

— Jean Vanier[1]

Old things made new

Our ancestors gathered around a fire in a circle. Families gather around the kitchen table in a circle. Now, we are learning to gather in a circle as a community to solve prob-lems, support one another, and connect to one another.

A new way of bringing people together to understand one another, strengthen bonds, and solve community prob-lems is blossoming in modern Western communities. But this new way is really very old. It draws on the ancient Na-tive American tradition of using a talking piece, an object passed from person to person in a group and which grants the holder sole permission to speak. It combines this an-cient tradition with contemporary concepts of democracy and inclusivity in a complex, multicultural society.

Peacemaking Circles are being used in a variety of con-texts. In neighborhoods they provide support for those harmed by crime and help decide sentences for those who commit crime. In schools, they create a positive classroom climate and resolve behavior problems. In the workplace, they help address conflict, and in social services they develop more organic support systems for people struggling to get their lives together.

Circles are being used in:

- neighborhoods
- schools
- workplaces
- social services
- justice systems

The Circle Process is a story-telling process. Every person has a story, and every story has a lesson to offer. In the Circle, people touch one another's lives by sharing stories that have meaning to them. As the following three vignettes suggest, stories unite people in their common humanity and help them appreciate the depth and beauty of the human experience.

• • •

A breathless first-grader runs up to the school administrator supervising the playground. "Mrs. Ticiu! Mrs. Ticiu!" he exclaims. "I need a talking piece!" Mrs. Ticiu reaches into her pocket, extracts a small plastic dinosaur, and offers it to the child. He grasps the dinosaur tightly in his fist and dashes off to join several other students who, moments earlier, were arguing. With the help of the talking piece, they discuss their disagreement and find a solution they all like.

• • •

Legislators, state policy analysts, state agency administrators, and youth workers sit at tables with adolescents who have gotten into trouble to discuss the state vision for delinquent youth in Minnesota. As a talking piece is passed around the table, each person gets an equal chance to hear and share perspectives. Everyone listens intently to each speaker. After thoughtful listening and discussion, each table reaches a consensus position regarding its assigned topic.

• • •

In an inner-city neighborhood, an adolescent and his mom sit in a Circle with nearly a dozen community members and justice system professionals, including a prosecutor and a public defender. The assembled group stands and joins hands to express gratitude for the opportunity to come together as a community to support this adolescent and his family. A talking piece is passed and introductions are made. Each welcomes the youth and his mother to the Circle.

As the talking pieces makes its second round, Circle participants ask the youth about his progress in school, his behavior at home, and his interests. Two members of the Circle have visited his school and offer to help him catch up with his schoolwork. The youth's mother expresses grave concern that he is leaving the house without her permission. She talks about her fears for him when he is out on the street after dark.

As the talking piece circulates among those present, Circle participants share fears and anxieties from their own adolescence. In dialogue with the youth, they express care and concern but also clear expectations about school attendance, homework, and checking in with Mom before leaving the house.

Both the youth and his mother respond warmly to the overtures of support and concern from the Circle. Both are able to listen to one another better with the use of the talking piece, and they leave with a better understanding of each other's concerns and frustrations.

The youth promises to comply with the agreement, and the group schedules another Circle meeting to check on his *progress. The group stands and joins hands for a closing acknowledgment of the hard work done.*

Peacemaking Circles like those described above are bringing people together as equals to have honest exchanges about difficult issues and painful experiences in an atmosphere of respect and concern for everyone. In increasingly varied settings, Peacemaking Circles are providing a space in which people from widely divergent perspectives can come together to speak candidly about conflict, pain, and anger and leave those conversations feeling good about themselves and about others.

> The philosphy of Circles acknowledges that we are all in need of help and that helping others helps us at the same time.

The underlying philosophy of Circles acknowledges that we are all in need of help and that helping others helps us at the same time. The participants of the Circle benefit from the collective wisdom of everyone in the Circle. Participants are not divided into givers and receivers: everyone is both a giver and a receiver. Circles draw on the life experience and wisdom of all participants to generate new understandings of the problem and new possibilities for solutions.

Peacemaking Circles bring together the ancient wisdom of community and the contemporary value of respect for individual gifts, needs, and differences in a process that:

- honors the presence and dignity of every participant
- values the contributions of every participant

- emphasizes the connectedness of all things
- supports emotional and spiritual expression
- gives equal voice to all

About this book

This book is an overview of Peacemaking Circles and is designed to familiarize readers with the general nature of the process, its underlying philosophy, and ways the Peacemaking Circle Process can be used. It is not a detailed description of the process nor does it explain how to conduct Circles in general.

The book will explain how to conduct a simple Talking Circle, but this is not adequate preparation for leading more complex Circles. Facilitating a Circle requires more than putting chairs in a circle. Training in Circle facilitation is recommended before attempting to conduct a Circle in circumstances involving conflict, strong emotions, or victimization.[2]

Historical context

Peacemaking Circles draw directly from the tradition of the Talking Circle, common among indigenous people of North America. Gathering in a Circle to discuss important community issues was likely a part of the tribal roots of most people. Such processes still exist among indigenous people around the world, and we are deeply indebted to those who have kept these practices alive as a source of wisdom and inspiration for modern Western cultures.

In contemporary society and largely outside the scope of mainstream awareness, Circles have been used by small groups of non-indigenous people for over 30 years. Women's groups in particular have made extensive use of a formal Circle Process. Those Circles have primarily occurred in the contexts of individuals sharing their personal journeys in a supportive community. Some individuals have taken their experience with personal Circles into public settings, but a systemic effort to use Circles in mainstream public processes, such as criminal justice, is relatively new and grows out of work undertaken in Yukon, Canada, in the early 1990s.

An overview of Circles

A Peacemaking Circle is a way of bringing people together in which:

- everyone is respected
- everyone gets a chance to talk without interruption
- participants explain themselves by telling their stories
- everyone is equal—no person is more important than anyone else
- spiritual and emotional aspects of individual experience are welcomed

Peacemaking Circles are useful when two or more people:

- need to make decisions together
- have a disagreement
- need to address an experience that resulted in harm to someone
- want to work together as a team
- wish to celebrate
- wish to share difficulties
- want to learn from each other

Introduction

> **The Peacemaking Circle is a container strong enough to hold:**
>
> - anger
> - frustration
> - joy
> - pain
> - truth
> - conflict
> - diverse world views
> - intense feelings
> - silence
> - paradox

This book is about Circle work that originated in public settings—Circles used more in a context of community-building than in a context of personal development, though all effective Circles ultimately engage people on a personal level, connect people in deep and personal places, and therefore contribute to personal development. In the United States, Peacemaking Circles were introduced under the philosophy of restorative justice, which promotes including all those impacted by a crime in a process of understanding the harm of crime and devising strategies for repairing the harm.[3]

The Peacemaking Circle Process in the United States began in the Minnesota criminal justice system. Peacemaking Circles offered a way to include those harmed by crime, those who commit crime, and the community in a partnership with the justice system to determine the most effective response to a crime that would promote healing and safety for everyone. The goals of the Circle include developing support for those harmed by crime, deciding the sentence for those who commit crime and supporting them in fulfilling the obligations of the sentence, and strengthening the community to prevent crimes.

Rural, suburban, and urban communities are using the process for criminal cases involving both adult and juvenile crimes. Peacemaking Circles are active across a range of cultural communities including African American, Euro-American, Hmong, Latino, Cambodian, and Native American.

> **Circle Processes are part of the roots of most traditions.**

Though Circles began in the context of the sentencing process, corrections practitioners found other applications for this approach within the criminal justice system. Innovative professionals began using Circles to facilitate community re-entry for people who have been incarcerated and to improve the effectiveness of community supervision for people on probation.

Circles in Minnesota began as a part of the criminal justice process but soon found use elsewhere. Community volunteers working in Justice Circle projects quickly recognized that the process would be helpful in many situations not related to crime, so they took Circles into schools, workplaces, social services, churches, neighborhood groups, and their families.

The spread of Peacemaking Circles has been spontaneous and organic, seeds carried from one place to another by passion and commitment more than by strategic planning or organized dissemination.

2.
Circles in Practice

"I'm impressed with the gentleness of the Circle.
It arrives at something in such a gentle way."
— Circle participant in an alternative school

How does a Peacemaking Circle work?

Peacemaking Circles use structure to create possibilities for freedom: freedom to speak our truth, freedom to drop masks and protections, freedom to be present as a whole human being, freedom to reveal our deepest longings, freedom to acknowledge mistakes and fears, freedom to act in accord with our core values.

Participants sit in a circle of chairs with no tables. Sometimes objects that have meaning to the group are placed in the center as a focal point to remind participants of shared values and common ground. The physical format of the Circle symbolizes shared leadership, equality, connection, and inclusion. It also promotes focus, accountability, and participation from all.

Using very intentional structural elements—ceremony, a talking piece, a facilitator or keeper, guidelines, and consensus decision-making—Circles aim to create a space in which participants are safe to be their most authentic self. (These elements, explained briefly here, are addressed more fully in Chapter 6.)

Ceremony—Circles consciously engage all aspects of human experience—spiritual, emotional, physical, and mental. Circles use a ceremony or intentional centering activity in the opening and in the closing to mark the Circle as a sacred space in which participants are present with themselves and one another in a way that is different from an ordinary meeting.

A Talking Piece—By allowing only the person holding the talking piece to speak, a Circle regulates the dialogue as the piece circulates consecutively from person to person around the group. The person holding the talking piece has the undivided attention of everyone else in the Circle and can speak without interruption. The use of the talking piece allows for full expression of emotions, deeper listening, thoughtful reflection, and an unhurried pace. Additionally, the talking piece creates space for people who find it difficult to speak in a group, but it never requires the holder to speak.

A Facilitator or Keeper—The facilitator of the Peacemaking Circle, often called a keeper, assists the group in creating and maintaining a collective space in which each participant feels safe to speak honestly and openly without disrespecting anyone else. The keeper monitors the quality of the collective space and stimulates the reflections of the group through questions or topic suggestions. The keeper does not control the issues raised by the group or try to move the group toward a particular outcome, but the keeper may take steps to address the tone of the group interaction.

Guidelines—Participants in a Circle play a major role in designing their own space by creating the guidelines for their discussion. The guidelines articulate the promises participants make to one another about how they will conduct themselves in the Circle dialogue. The guidelines are intended to describe the behaviors that the participants feel will make the space safe for them to speak their truth. Guidelines are not rules and they are not used to judge people's behavior. They are used as gentle reminders to participants about their shared commitment to creating a safe space for difficult conversation.

Consensus Decision-Making—Decisions in a Circle are made by consensus. Consensus does not require enthusiasm for the decision or plan, but it does require that each participant is willing to live with the decision and support its implementation.

In a Circle, relationship-building and getting to know one another beyond the context of the task precede discussion about the task itself. Half the time of a Circle may be spent on creating the foundation for deeply honest dialogue about the conflict or difficulty before that dialogue begins. Discussing values, creating guidelines, and sharing unseen aspects of ourselves are all part of creating the foundation for dialogue that engages participants' spirits and emotions as well as their intellect.

> Wisdom in a Circle is accessed through personal stories.

Wisdom in a Circle is accessed through personal stories. In a Circle, life experience is more valuable than advice. Participants share their experiences of joy and pain, struggle and triumph, vulnerability and strength to understand the issue at hand. Because storytelling engages people on many levels—emotional, spiritual, physical, and mental—listeners absorb stories differently than they do advice.

Types of Peacemaking Circles

As Circles found various uses, a terminology emerged to distinguish the different types of Circles by their function. This language is still developing and the terms are not universally used, but they are still helpful.

Types of Circles include:

- Talking
- Understanding
- Healing
- Sentencing
- Support
- Community-Building
- Conflict
- Reintegration
- Celebration

Talking Circles—In a Talking Circle, participants explore a particular issue or topic from many different perspectives. Talking Circles do not attempt to reach consensus on the topic. Rather, they allow all voices to be respectfully heard and offer participants diverse perspectives to stimulate their reflections.

Circles of Understanding—A Circle of Understanding is a Talking Circle focused on understanding some aspect of a conflict or difficult situation. A Circle of Understanding is generally not a decision-making Circle; therefore, it does not need to reach consensus. Its purpose is to develop a more complete picture of the context or reason for a particular event or behavior.

Healing Circles—The purpose of a Healing Circle is to share the pain of a person or persons who have experienced trauma or loss. A plan for support beyond the Circle may emerge, but it is not required.

A tenth-grade student was referred to Circle for school attendance issues. In addition, he had also been in trouble for smoking. During the second Circle, he told a story about how he had not felt comfortable in school since being expelled in the fall of his eighth-grade year for the remainder of that year.

No one at the high school had any idea how traumatic the experience was for him until both he and his mother talked about it in the Circle. He told the members that this was the first time since the eighth grade that he felt anyone at school had really tried to understand where he was coming from.[4]

Sentencing Circles—A Sentencing Circle is a community-directed process in partnership with the criminal justice system. It involves all those affected by an offense in deciding an appropriate sentencing plan which addresses the concerns of all participants.

This Circle brings together the person who has been harmed, the person who caused the harm, family and friends of each, other community members, justice system representatives (judge, prosecutor, defense counsel, police, probation officer), and other resource professionals. The participants discuss: 1) what happened, 2) why it happened, 3) what the impact is, and 4) what is needed to repair the harm and prevent it from happening again.

By consensus, the Circle develops the sentence for the person who committed the crime and may also stipulate responsibilities of community members and justice officials as part of the agreement. Preparation for a Sentencing Circle may involve a Healing Circle for the person harmed and a Circle of Understanding for the one who committed the harm before bringing the two parties together.

Support Circles—A Support Circle brings together key people to support a person through a particular difficulty or major change in life. Support Circles often meet regularly over a period of time. By consensus, Support Circles may develop agreements or plans, but they are not necessarily decision-making Circles.

Community-Building Circles—The purpose of a Community-Building Circle is to create bonds and build relationships among a group of people who have a shared interest. Community-Building Circles support effective collective action and mutual responsibility.

Conflict Circles—A Conflict Circle brings together disputing parties to resolve their differences. Resolution takes shape through a consensus agreement.

Reintegration Circles—Reintegration Circles bring together an individual and a group or community from which that individual has been estranged to work toward reconciliation and acceptance of the individual into the group again. Reintegration Circles frequently develop consensus agreements. They have been used for juveniles and adults who are returning to the community from prisons or correctional facilities.

Celebration or Honoring Circles—Celebration Circles bring together a group of people to recognize an individual or a group and to share joy and a sense of accomplishment.

Applications of Peacemaking Circles

Peacemaking Circles have been used for the following:

- Supporting and assisting victims of crime
- Criminal sentencing for juveniles and adults
- Reintegrating inmates into communities upon leaving prison
- Supporting and monitoring chronic offenders on probation
- Providing support for families accused of child abuse and neglect, while keeping the child safe
- Team-building and staff renewal in social service agencies
- Developing mission statements and strategic plans within organizations
- Developing new programs in an agency
- Handling discrimination, harassment, and interpersonal conflicts within the workplace
- Addressing neighborhood disagreements
- Managing classrooms and playground conflicts

- Handling school discipline
- Teaching writing in an alternative school
- Repairing harms inflicted by a sixth-grade class on a substitute teacher
- Processing chemical dependency relapses in a high school for recovering addicts
- Developing education plans for special education students
- Resolving family conflicts
- Grieving losses in a family or community
- Handling environmental and planning disputes
- Facilitating dialogue between immigrant communities and local government
- Facilitating dialogue between rival gangs
- Leading college classes discussions
- Celebrating graduations and birthdays
- Discussing youth presence at a suburban mall

3.
A Circle Story—
Finding a Way to Move Forward After a Worker Strike[4]

In the aftermath of a polarizing state workers' strike, administrators of a juvenile residential facility took a proactive stance by suggesting that a Circle be called. They hoped this would be a way to get the issues out in the open, allow people to share their stories, create a safe place for feelings to be shared and heard, express what was needed to move on, and to start the healing process.

Our plan was to have a half-day Circle to introduce the process and to set parameters for what could be done to help the agency through this time. This would serve as an opportunity to begin the healing process and to prepare individuals for the second Circle, which would focus more on the emotional issues at the root of the tensions.

A week after this first Circle, we set aside an entire day for a second Circle to deal with the core issues that individuals were struggling with. From the beginning, we acknowledged that these two sessions would likely only be the start of a long process, and that the Circle keepers were neither experts nor problem-solvers, but were present to be support people in guiding the agency through the process.

First Circle

We spent substantial time framing the process and setting the stage for the work we would be doing together. To guide the Circle, we placed the residential program's guiding principles and core values in the center to remind participants of their commitment to help kids. This was important as the team created and voted on these guiding principles and core values, so that they held weight within the work culture. We also asked everyone to imagine a larger circle of students encircling our own, watching the adults model mature problem-solving and serving as a reminder of what is truly important to their purpose of working at this program.

We emphasized and modeled the Circle Process as a safe place to share and hopefully heal, and stressed that this was different than a "staff meeting" or a "mediation session." We did this by working to create a "sacred space" where individuals would be able to listen and speak from the heart, have the right to remain silent, commit to confidentiality, and to respect the talking piece by ensuring that the holder of the piece would be the only person speaking at any one time.

By working to create a sense of ceremony through opening and closing readings/meditations and other rituals, we emphasized the importance of creating a space that was conducive for this type of work. We also emphasized that the group was just as much responsible for co-facilitation as we were as Circle keepers. It was our belief that if we spent significant time and energy introducing the process and setting a tone, we would hopefully nurture an environment in which people would over time become comfortable in being honest with themselves and others.

The first few rounds of the talking piece centered on introductions, "check-ins," and lighthearted questions designed to relax the group and to build some universality among participants. The next round asked Circle members to share what they needed to feel safe through this process. This question was important in order to get people to think in general terms about what they need to feel safe, and also for other Circle members to develop an awareness of how their behavior could potentially impact others.

The next round consisted of an activity in which Circle members were asked to record on an index card how the strike impacted them personally. Individuals were asked to write down if they believed they were harmed by anyone during the strike, and also if they knowingly inflicted harm on anyone. After they finished writing, they were asked to place their index cards in a safe place until we met again, and if they chose to do so, they would then have an opportunity to share their reflections.

This activity was designed so participants would reflect on their personal behavior, as well as explore the impact on self, family, and work relationships that occurred as a result of the strike. We concluded the first Circle by asking participants to share what their hopes were for the residential program and for themselves in the next three months.

Overall, the tone of the first Circle was positive despite the clear tension that existed among participants. It was clear that people wanted to maintain their positive work with kids and valued that above all else. However, there were conflicting views about how to move on after the strike due to deep-seated views on labor unions, individual responses to stress, and current levels of anger. It appeared that some individuals were ready to get into difficult issues right away, while others were very worried about what could happen during the Circle.

Some participants were grateful that a Circle was being held to address the issue, and others claimed not to believe in the process and verbalized their belief that it was a waste of time. Despite the diversity of expectations toward the process, we believed that we were able to set the stage for the following Circle.

Second Circle

After initiating the Circle with an opening reading, we reviewed what we had done in the previous session, emphasizing the program's guiding principles and core values that were at the center of the Circle. Again we asked the group to imagine a larger circle of clients around us that would hopefully keep the group focused on the big picture.

The first pass of the talking piece consisted of a "check-in" where participants were asked to share how they were doing in general terms and also how they felt about returning to the Circle. The next round centered on exploring what was the most stressful thing for individuals and their families during the strike. Both of these rounds took a substantial amount of time as group members spoke eloquently about their experience of stress during the strike, and also about the residual stress as a result of actions that transpired during that time.

The next round gave participants a chance to share their individual impact statements they had written the previous week. This was an emotional round for many as they shared in detail how they believed they were impacted, how they perceived they were harmed, and/or how they believed they may have harmed their co-workers through their actions.

At the next round we asked the Circle to share what they needed in order to "move on." People shared that they needed a variety of things, including time, patience, understanding, forgiveness, etc. Since many people made apologies during the previous round, we encouraged people to make amends or set plans to address harms during this round.

After doing a good job of articulating what they needed to heal, we transitioned to having Circle participants make commitments about what they as individuals would do to help the program move forward and function in a safe and healthy manner. Again, most people were positive and hopeful and made strong commitments to help the program through this time and to maintain the high quality programming that the facility provides to adolescent boys.

4.
Foundations of Circles

"In every one of us there is a deep desire
to connect to others in a good way."
— Judge Barry Stuart, Yukon, Canada

Values

Peacemaking Circles are not a neutral, value-free
process. Rather, they are consciously built on a foundation of shared values. A specific set of values is not pre-
scribed for Circles, but the value framework is the same
for all Circles.

Circles assume a universal human wish to be connected to others in a good way. The values of a Circle derive
from this basic human impulse. Therefore values that nurture and promote good connections to others are the foundation of the Circle.

There is no single "right" way to express those values,
and even though in my experience those values are similar across different groups, they cannot be taken for grant-
ed. Peacemaking Circles are intentional and explicit in
identifying values before entering dialogue about issues.
Because the Circle asks all participants to act on those values within the Circle to the best of their ability, Circle participants must truly claim the values.

Peacemaking Circles: From Crime to Community suggests
the following values as foundational for Circles: respect,

honesty, humility, sharing, courage, inclusivity, empathy, trust, forgiveness and love.[6] Community Circles of Washington County, Minnesota, identified the following values as the basis of their Circles: respect, humility, compassion, spirituality, and honesty.

Many people believe that young people who get in trouble do not share these values. However, a group of juveniles incarcerated in a correctional facility created a list for their Circle that included respect, openmindedness, responsibility, caring, honesty, and hearing each other's point of view.

These examples illustrate both the common value framework (values that nurture and promote a good connection to others) and the diverse ways that groups may put into words what guides their behavior. When participants consciously choose the values they want to guide their interaction, they are much more deliberate about keeping their behavior aligned with those values. A participant in a pain-filled, gut-wrenching Circle named self-control as the value he wanted to put in the Circle. Later in the Circle he stated, "I'm just glad I put self-control in the Circle because otherwise I wouldn't be using it now."

> Circles assume a universal human wish to be connected to others in a good way.

Ancient teachings

In addition to the values associated with humans being their "best selves," the foundation of the Circle Process includes several assumptions about the nature of the universe. These assumptions are common in the worldview of most indigenous cultures and are often metaphorically associated with the image of the Circle. These assumptions have been passed from generation to generation through cultural teachings.

One of the most important teachings underlying the Circle Process is the assertion that everything in the universe is connected. This teaching tells us that every action affects everything in the universe, that it is impossible to isolate something to act on it without affecting everything else. In this worldview there is no such thing as an objective observer or a detached perspective. Everything is connected.

> We need the person for whom the Circle is formed just as much as that person needs us.

A corollary to this assumption is the understanding that we cannot just "get rid of" our problems. An educator, overhearing a group of people talking about restorative justice, exclaimed, "Oh, I get it. Just like 30 years ago when we threw a bottle out the window, we thought we threw it 'away,' and then the environmental movement taught us there is no 'away.' This is the same for people."

When we operate under the illusion that we can throw something away, it comes back to poison us in a way that we may not realize because we have assumed that it is gone. Circles hold at their center the importance of recognizing the impact of our behavior on others and acknowledging the interconnectedness of our fates. Harm to one is harm to all. Good for one is good for all.

Another corollary to this teaching about connection is the assumption that we are interdependent, that we need each other in fundamental ways. A community member in a Circle for a person who committed a crime observed:

What I gotta do to keep what I got is to give it away. I need to be in Circle. When I'm by myself, it doesn't go so good. People come together and work together to try to help each other. Gotta give it away to keep it. It's just the way it works.

The assumption of the Circle is that we need the person for whom the Circle is formed just as much as that person needs us.

Because we all are connected and all are interdependent, each of us has value to the whole. Therefore, Circles operate from the belief that each person has inherent dignity and worth. We all equally deserve respect and the opportunity to voice our perspectives.

This belief that everything is connected, that there is no objective observer, and that we are profoundly interdependent is now powerfully supported by quantum physics. Margaret J. Wheatley in her book *Leadership and the New Science* describes how the shift from a Newtonian understanding of the universe to a quantum understanding is just now, a century after the key discoveries, being incorporated into thinking about human relationships and organizations in Western society.[7]

She writes:

Each of us lives and works in organizations designed from Newtonian images of the universe. . . Things can be taken apart, dissected literally or representationally (as we have done with business functions and academic disciplines), and then put back together without any significant loss. The assumption is that by comprehending the workings of each piece, the whole can be understood. The Newtonian model of the world is characterized by materialism and reductionism—a focus on things rather than relationships.[8]

In comparison, Wheatley explains the quantum view:

The quantum mechanical view of reality strikes against most of our notions of reality . . . It is a world where *relationship* is the key determiner of what is observed . . . Particles come into being and are observed only in relationship to something else. They do not exist as independent "things." . . . These unseen *connections* between what were previously thought to be separate entities are the fundamental elements of all creation.[9]

Community Building

Healing

Connections

Circle Keeping
Talking Piece
Guidelines
Ceremony
Consensus

Shared Values

Ancient Teachings

Guidance of Medicine
Wheel Teachings

Perhaps that level of interconnectedness is not familiar to Western cultures, but it is familiar to many indigenous cultures. And thus, ancient wisdom and modern science, coming from two different ways of knowing and vastly different cultures, arrive at the same conclusion. Though modern physics and ancient metaphysics reach the same conclusions, this belief is not at the foundation of many Western social structures that are built on a Newtonian model of objective reality and separable components.

Another ancient teaching foundational for Circles is that human experience has mental, physical, emotional, and spiritual aspects. All of these aspects of human experience are equally important and offer essential gifts to our collective life. Balance among these aspects is important for the health of individuals and communities. Consequently, Circles intentionally create a space in which all of these aspects of human experience are recognized and welcomed.

Emotional and spiritual expressions that reflect the personal perspective of the speaker, but are not assumed to be the same for others, have a place in the Circle. Circles assume that conflicts and difficulties have emotional and spiritual content for participants and that effective resolutions require exploring the emotional and spiritual content as well as the physical and mental content.

Circle Process as practiced in faith-based communities

Thomas W. Porter Jr., Executive Director of JUSTPEACE

Inspired by the work of Kay Pranis, the JUSTPEACE Center for Mediation and Conflict Transformation in the United Methodist Church has found the Circle Process a great gift to the Church. We have found that it:

- Evokes the best of our theology.
- Recognizes the importance of ritual and sacred space and time.
- Emphasizes the significance of relational covenants.
- Encourages deep listening and respectful speaking from the heart.
- Moves us away from parliamentary procedure to consensus decision-making.
- Creates an empowering servant or stewardship understanding of leadership.
- Focuses us on the mission of reconciliation, healing relationships, and creating community.

In short, the Circle Process has helped bring us back to a better and more faithful way of being Church. As the Process gained wide acceptance, we have found that it has the capacity to transform the way we make decisions, the way we conduct our grievance procedures, even the way we experience Holy Communion as the ritual of reconciliation and the healing of relationships.

5.
A Circle Story—
Finding Understanding
in the Classroom[10]

A student in an elementary school threatened to burn down the school following recess. This incident occurred soon after the school shootings in Littleton, Colorado, and his anger sparked fear among his classmates.

The teacher requested a Circle of Understanding for the students, and the next day the entire classroom participated in it. During the Circle, students expressed their feelings about how the threats had impacted them. Many of the students reported experiencing nightmares as a result of the student's threat. The students also reflected on how their own behavior had an effect on the student who made the threat and how they were responsible, to a degree, for his behavior.

At the conclusion of the Circle, the boy agreed to make changes in his own behavior by: 1) not swearing or threatening others, 2) thinking before speaking, and 3) walking away when he was mad to cool down and then talking it out later. He also agreed to write an apology letter to his classmates.

His classmates agreed to make changes in their behavior by: 1) being nicer to him, 2) not telling lies about him,

3) not teasing him, 4) playing with him so he would have more friends, 5) being his partner in class, 6) helping him make new friends, 7) sticking up for him in a good way, 8) forgiving him and giving him a second chance, and 9) playing basketball with him after school.

A previous behavior contract with the boy banned him from the playground for the rest of the school year. His classmates did not want that to happen; instead, they wanted to give him another chance. They felt that if everyone did what he/she agreed to in the Circle, there would be no more problems on the playground. They were right. The boy was given a second chance to play on the playground with his classmates, and he followed through on the conditions of the agreement.

6.
Key Elements of Circles

Structural elements of Circles

Building on the foundation of values and ancient teachings, Circles use five key structural elements to create a safe space for people to connect with others in a good way, even in circumstances of conflict, harm, or difficulty. These elements include ceremony, guidelines, a talking piece, keeping/facilitation, and consensus decision-making.

Ceremony

Opening and closing ceremonies mark the time and space of the Circle as a space apart. It is a distinctly different space because the Circle invites people to be in touch with the value of connecting deeply with others, and it encourages people to drop the ordinary masks and protections that create distance from others.

Opening ceremonies help participants shift gears from the pace and tone of ordinary life to the pace and tone of the Circle. Opening ceremonies help participants to center themselves, be reminded of core values, clear negative energies from unrelated stresses, encourage a sense of optimism, and honor the presence of everyone there.

Closing ceremonies acknowledge the efforts of the Circle, affirm the interconnectedness of those present, convey a sense of hope for the future, and prepare participants to return to the ordinary space of their lives. Opening and closing ceremonies are designed to fit the nature of the particular group and provide opportunities for cultural responsiveness.

Guidelines

The guidelines of the Circle are the commitments or promises that participants make to one another about how they will behave in the Circle. The purpose of the guidelines is to establish clear expectations for conduct based on what the participants need to make the space safe to speak in their authentic voices, and to act from the impulse to be connected to others in a good way. Guidelines are designed to meet the needs of the specific Circle and always include respectful speaking and listening and some form of confidentiality.

> Guidelines are adopted by consensus of the Circle.

The entire Circle, not just the facilitator, is responsible for the creation and implementation of the guidelines. Guidelines are not rigid constraints but supportive reminders of the behavioral expectations of everyone in the Circle. They are not imposed on the participants but rather are adopted by consensus of the Circle.

Developing guidelines begins during the preparation phase and continues when the Circle convenes. If someone disagrees with a proposed guideline, the keeper facilitates a discussion exploring the purpose of the guideline and the concern raised. It is a search for understanding and for common ground to ensure a space that is respectful for all participants.

It is generally not difficult to reach consensus on the guidelines. For example, even in circumstances of hostility, when parties may not value hearing each other, they still want respectful listening as a guideline because *they* wish to be heard respectfully. The guidelines arise out of asking people what they want *for* themselves *from* others and then, naturally, those guidelines apply to everyone in the Circle.

Discussion of guidelines helps Circle participants reflect on how they will be present with one another so they can act more intentionally than they might otherwise, especially in circumstances of conflict or anger.

Talking Piece

The talking piece is an object that is passed from person to person around the Circle. As its name implies, the holder of the talking piece has the opportunity to talk while all other participants have the opportunity to listen without thinking about a response. The holder of the talking piece may also choose to offer silence, or the holder may pass the piece without speaking. There is no obligation to speak when the talking piece comes.

The talking piece is a critical element of creating a space in which participants can speak from a deep place of truth. It assures speakers that they will not be interrupted, that they will be able to pause and find the words that express what is on their hearts and minds, that they will be fully and respectfully heard. The talking piece slows the pace of conversation and encourages thoughtful and reflective interactions among participants. It often carries symbolic meaning related to the group's shared values and thus is a concrete reminder to the speaker of those values.

The talking piece creates a level of order in the dialogue that allows the expression of difficult emotions without the process spinning out of control. Because only one person can speak at a time and the talking piece moves in order around the Circle, two people cannot go back and forth at each other when they disagree or are angry. The talking piece spreads the responsibility around the Circle for responding to and managing the difficult feelings. Because Circle participants know the keeper usually will not speak until the talking piece reaches him/her, others in the Circle often respond in mediating ways to expressions of pain, anger, or conflict.

> The talking piece is a critical element of creating a space in which participants can speak from a deep place of truth.

The talking piece is a powerful equalizer. It allows every participant an equal opportunity to speak and carries an implicit assumption that every participant has something important to offer the group. The talking piece facilitates the contributions of quiet people who are unlikely to assert themselves in a typical open dialogue. As it passes physically from hand to hand, the talking piece weaves a connecting thread among the members of the Circle.

Keeping/Facilitation

The term "keeper" is commonly used for the facilitator of the Circle. Thomas Porter, director of the United Methodist JUSTPEACE organization, uses the term "steward" when conducting Circles within Christian settings. In this book, I use keeper and facilitator interchangeably. The keeper in a Circle is not responsible for finding solutions or for controlling the group. The keeper's role is to initiate a space that is respectful and safe, and to engage participants in sharing responsibility for the space and for their shared work.

The keeper helps the group access its individual and collective wisdom by opening the space in a careful way and monitoring the quality of the space as the group proceeds. The large role played by the talking piece in regulating the dialogue reduces the role of the keeper as a facilitator relative to other dialogue processes. The keeper may speak without the talking piece but rarely does so.

The role of the keeper is not that of a "neutral," common in Western conflict resolution models. The keeper is a participant in the process and may offer her thoughts, ideas, and stories. Minimizing bias in the facilitator is still a goal of the Circle Process, but this is achieved through caring about everyone in the Circle rather than by holding a clinical distance.

Because guidelines in a Circle are created by consensus of the group and belong to the group, the keeper is not an enforcer but a monitor. If the guidelines are not working, then the keeper draws the attention of the group to the need to address guidelines.[11] Except for small Circles, it is common to have two keepers facilitating a Circle. One of the most important characteristics of an effective keeper is the ability to let go of control, to share responsibility for both the process and the outcomes with the participants of the Circle.

Consensus Decision-Making

Not all Peacemaking Circles make decisions, but when they do, the decisions are made by consensus. Consensus in the Circle Process is generally understood to mean that all participants are willing to live with the decision and support its implementation.

Consensus decision-making is grounded in a deep commitment to understand the needs and interests of all participants and to work toward meeting all of those needs. It requires deep listening and reflection before making decisions. A commitment to consensus engages participants in helping others meet their needs while also meeting the participant's own needs. Consensus challenges participants to speak truthfully if they cannot live with a decision, and then to help the group find a solution they can live with that meets the needs of the group as well.

Entering a consensus process requires an attitude of exploration rather than of conquering or persuading. The deep and respectful listening to all participants resulting from the use of the talking piece makes consensus decision-making a natural outcome of the Circle Process.

Consensus is not always possible, but it is a rare experience not to reach consensus in a Circle if adequate time is allowed to hear fully all perspectives.

Consensus gives power to everyone.

When participants feel fully heard and observe that the Circle tried to address their needs, they rarely block consensus, even if they do not get what they wanted in a particular decision.

If consensus cannot be reached, the decision can revert to whatever process would normally apply. Generally, there will be much richer information available to that process as a result of the Circle.

Consensus decisions produce more effective and sustainable agreements because consensus-based processes give power to everyone. Achieving consensus requires the group to pay attention to the interests of those who are normally powerless. Consensus processes hold the potential for more fundamentally democratic results because all interests must be taken into account. Decisions must ultimately represent everyone involved or consensus will not be achieved. Therefore, decisions must address the interests of everyone to some degree.

Decisions or plans addressing the interests of all participants have a far greater likelihood of success because every participant has something to gain by successful completion of the agreement. Consequently, every participant has an investment in success. Decision-making by consensus generally takes more time in the decision-making process but less time in implementation because of the commitment of all parties to the decision.

These five structural elements—ceremony, guidelines, a talking piece, a keeper, and consensus decision-making constructed on the foundation of shared values and indigenous teachings—create a "container" in which people can draw on the best in themselves to reach out to one another and connect at profound levels.

The importance of storytelling

Story-telling delivers information in a way that opens the listener. When information is asserted or presented cognitively, we immediately engage a screening device to determine whether we agree or disagree. We are primarily engaged mentally and begin thinking about how we will respond.

Storytelling employs a different kind of listening. The body relaxes, settles back, is more open and less anxious. We take in the story before screening the content. We are engaged emotionally as well as mentally. This different kind of listening allows information to be exchanged more thoroughly, leading to much greater understanding between people.

Circles are a storytelling process. They use the history and experience of everyone in the Circle to understand the situation and to look for a good way forward—not through lecturing or giving advice or telling others what to do, but through sharing stories of struggle, pain, joy, despair, and triumph. Personal narratives are the source of insight and wisdom in Circles.

By sharing our individual stories we open places for others to connect to us, to find common ground with us, and to know us more completely. In a respectful speaker/listener relationship, both individuals open themselves to a deeper connection to the other. When people share stories of pain or mistakes and drop layers of protection, revealing themselves as struggling, vulnerable human beings, we feel more connected to them. It becomes much harder to hold someone as the distant "other" and not feel connected to that person through our common humanity. It becomes more difficult to hold anger or fear or disinterest toward someone who shares pain and vulnerability. Unless we are already familiar with the life history of the speaker, sharing stories of pain and vulnerability usually shatters some assumption we have made about the person telling the story.

> Storytelling strengthens a sense of connectedness, fosters self-reflection, and empowers participants.

Telling our stories is a process of self-reflection. In telling our stories we articulate how we understand what has happened to us, why and how it has impacted us, and how we see ourselves and others. Our way of constructing our stories, which shapes our view of reality, becomes more transparent to us when we speak the story out loud to others.

To feel connected and respected, people need to tell their stories and have others listen. Having others listen to your story is a function of power in our culture. The more power you have, the more people will listen respectfully to your story. To listen respectfully to a person's story is to honor that person's intrinsic worth and to empower the storyteller in a constructive way.

Focusing on relationships

Before trying to work out issues or move to action, the Circle Process must first spend time helping participants connect as human beings. Harold Gatensby, a Tlingit First Nations Circle teacher and mentor from Carcross, Yukon, has applied the Medicine Wheel framework of four equal sections or elements to the Circle Process. (See diagram on p. 42.) The teaching of this Medicine Wheel image is that as much time must be spent on getting acquainted and building understanding as is spent on discussing the issues and making action plans.

Getting acquainted at a deeper level and building relationships happens primarily within the Circle itself. The early rounds of the Circle create ways for people to talk about who they are and what is important to them, and to share significant life experiences. These early rounds deliberately do not focus on the issues of contention.

The introduction round often invites people to share something meaningful about themselves. A values round may ask people to name a value they would like to bring to the Circle and why that value is important to them. A storytelling round in a Conflict Circle might invite participants to share an experience in which they had caused harm to another, but then resolved it in a way they felt good about. In these rounds the keepers model the vulnerability of sharing deep feelings. The rounds are posed toward positive sharing.

The Four Relational Elements of Circles
(based on the Medicine Wheel)

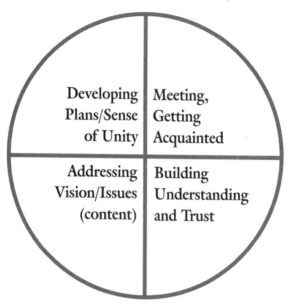

As participants reveal unknown or unseen aspects of themselves from a positive orientation, the negative assumptions others may make about them begin to crack and gradually lose strength. As participants share stories, they discover unexpected ways in which they are alike.

Careful preparation, hospitality when people arrive, a thoughtful opening, collective creation of guidelines, and the use of the talking piece all contribute to creating a space in which people are more likely to risk being vulnerable in the storytelling rounds. Once people are vulnerable with one another, trust begins to build. The level of connectedness and trust directly impacts the effectiveness of the discussion of issues and the development of plans to address the issues.

If a group of people has not developed a sense of connection and trust, discussion of issues often remains at a superficial level. People may not feel safe to speak their deepest truth if they do not have a sense of common ground that comes from knowing others beyond the usual introductions.

There is often a sense of great vulnerability in speaking the truth about difficult issues. Without a sense of trust and connection, people also will not be as quick to offer their gifts or resources that might serve the group's work. Plans that are developed based on a superficial level of information and analysis are ineffective.

A slight, nervous, 20-year-old male sat in the large circle of mostly middle-aged teachers, community members, and criminal justice professionals participating in a training on the Circle Process. The young man had been working with a local Criminal Justice Circle group for nearly a year. He had twice been through treatment for his addictions, particularly to methamphetamines, because of relapses, and recently lost his job because of a positive urine test for drugs. In spite of that, the Circle members who knew him welcomed him warmly with hugs.

As the talking piece came to him in the closing round for the day, he spoke directly and clearly, apologizing to the teachers in the room for the problems he had caused when he was in high school. Looking up from the feather, he spoke with deep conviction, "If it weren't for Circle and for all the caring and support and the wisdom of Circle, I'd be dead. There's so much love and support here. That's way cool. I can feel it right here" (pointing to his heart).[12]

When the plans fail to achieve the desired outcomes, groups typically go back to analyzing the problem and try a new plan. If they still have not built relationships and trust, they still will not get the deeper truth, and the analysis and plan will again fall short of the desired outcomes. Though the relationship-building takes time, it may in the end be more efficient because it supports the creation of effective and sustainable solutions.

Circles use the deep desire to be connected to others in a good way as a platform for developing relationships. That then enables people to probe issues in a more profound way, resulting in more profound resolutions to difficult problems or conflicts.

Stages of Circle Processes

As mentioned earlier, using Peacemaking Circles requires more than arranging chairs in a circle. Circles addressing conflict or harm involve a multi-stage process, and each stage is important for the effectiveness of the process. The four stages in most Circle Processes include determining suitability, preparation, convening the Circle, and follow-up.

Stage 1: Determining suitability. This involves assessing whether the Circle is an appropriate process for this situation by asking these questions:

- Are key parties willing to participate?
- Are trained facilitators available?
- Will the situation allow the time required to use the Circle Process?
- Can physical and emotional safety be maintained?

Stage 2: Preparation

- Identify who needs to participate: Who has been impacted? Who has resources, skills, or knowledge that might be needed? Who has similar life experiences that might add insight?
- Familiarize key parties with the process.
- Begin exploring the context of the issue.

Stage 3: Convening all parties

- Identify shared values and develop guidelines.
- Engage storytelling to build relationships and connections.
- Share concerns and hopes.
- Express feelings.
- Probe underlying causes of conflict or harm.
- Generate ideas for addressing harm or resolving conflict.

- Determine areas of consensus for action.
- Develop agreement and clarify responsibilities.

Stage 4: Follow-up

- Assess progress on agreements. Are all parties fulfilling their obligations?
- Probe for causes of any failure to fulfill an obligation, clarify responsibilities, and identify next steps if the failure continues.
- Adjust agreements as needed based on new information or developments.
- Celebrate successes.

Clearly Stage 3, convening all the parties, will be conducted in a Circle. However, Circles may also be used in the other three stages of the overall process. For example, when a Peacemaking Circle is used for sentencing in a criminal case, the process uses Circles in the steps leading to the actual Sentencing Circle:

• *Stage 1.* The offender may apply to the Circle Process through an Application Circle or Interview Circle.

• *Stage 2.* Preparation may include: a) creation of a support system for the offender, b) creation of a support system for the victim, c) Healing Circle(s) for the victim, d) Circle(s) of Understanding for the offender.

• *Stage 3.* The sentencing process is done in a Circle.

• *Stage 4.* Follow-up Circles may be used at appropriate intervals to review progress on the sentencing agreement.

7.
A Circle Story—
Finding Healing from a Violent Crime[13]

Laughter, hugs, and good-byes filled the air as people milled around the living room of a house in North Minneapolis. An exchange near the doorway of the house told the story of the evening.

"Are you still afraid?" asked a community member.

"No, I will not be afraid again," replied the man in his fifties.

This exchange followed a Peacemaking Circle in which the victim of an armed robbery met with the 17-year-old juvenile who had held a loaded gun to his head in his back yard. In the Circle were the victim's family, a friend, the juvenile's family, numerous community members, and juvenile justice professionals—about 20 people in all. The victim described the trauma of the crime and its impact on his life. The juvenile and his family expressed their regret and concern for the victim. Community members expressed support for both families and a hope that the community can come together to strengthen the neighborhood.

After everyone had a chance to speak, the victim asked to speak again. He looked across the circle of chairs at the juvenile and said, "When you get out of Red Wing (the juvenile correctional facility), I'd like to take you out to lunch."

A short time later, when a break was called in the process, the juvenile approached the victim's son of the same age with an outstretched hand. The son rose from his chair and hugged the juvenile. The juvenile then approached the victim and his wife, who also hugged him. The trauma of the previous six months was transformed into an experience of community support and expressions of remorse for the harm caused to the man and his family.

Before this Circle brought the two families together, separate Circles were held for the victim and the juvenile. The Circle of Understanding for the victim provided an opportunity for the victim to fully express the horror of the experience and its aftermath, including painful remarks by others suggesting that it was no big deal because "nobody got hurt."

Both families felt isolated and alone in their pain before the Circle Process. Neither family felt that the community cared about what was happening to them. Both families expressed surprise at the offers of help and support from community members who had no direct connection to the event. The Circle Process was able to break the cycle of isolation and fear. It gave participants a sense of hope about their future as a community beyond this individual case.

The dialogue of the Circle also brought to the surface important perspectives not often heard. The father and older brother of the juvenile were emphatic in their denunciation of guns. The older brother of the juvenile spoke in eloquent terms about the struggle of growing up as a young black male. Giving voice to these perspectives and raising community and system awareness is an important outcome of the Circle Process.

8.
Organizing a Talking Circle

Sitting in on a Circle is a wonderful way to learn more about the process. If there is no existing Circle available, organizing a Talking Circle is a good place to start. Training and personal healing work are essential before facilitating Circles around interpersonal conflict, trauma, difficult group decisions, or intensely emotional situations. However, it is possible to facilitate a Talking Circle without formal training.

Talking Circles do not attempt to bring a group to consensus or repair serious disruptions in relationships. They simply allow everyone to speak about a particular topic from his or her perspective. Sharing perspectives increases everyone's understanding of the issue and may improve relationships, but a Talking Circle would not attempt to do deep relationship work.

Talking Circles can be used to:

- Check in with one another in an ongoing group (class, staff, civic organization, committee, advisory board, project group).
- Reflect on a group experience such as a movie, video, speaker, or book.
- Give feedback to a leader or facilitator of a group process.

- Provide input to decision makers.
- Dialogue about community or social concerns such as racism.
- Explore different meanings of an experience or event for people.
- Share intergenerational perspectives.
- Exchange divergent points of view on an emotional topic such as gay marriage or abortion.

The following section will describe how to organize a Talking Circle around a community concern. The community could be a workplace, school, church, or neighborhood.

Begin by choosing a topic for the Circle. The topic should be something of keen interest for you as the organizer. Frame a statement of intent for the Talking Circle: What is the purpose of the Talking Circle? Then work through the four stages of the Circle Process as follows.

Stage 1: Suitability

Assess the suitability of the Talking Circle Process for the identified purpose by answering the following questions:

- Are there people who are willing to participate—does the topic matter to anyone? If not, then a Circle is *not* appropriate.
- Am I (the organizer) hoping to convince others of a particular point of view or change others? If the answer is yes, the Circle is *not* the appropriate forum.
- Am I open to hearing and respecting perspectives very different from mine? If not, then a Circle is *not* appropriate.
- Is the intent respectful of all possible participants? If not, then a Circle is *not* appropriate.

Stage 2: Preparation

After determining that a Talking Circle is a suitable forum for the dialogue you are interested in, begin preparations:

- Identify possible participants, making sure to include people with a variety of perspectives. The potential benefit of a Circle is dramatically reduced if all participants already view the topic the same way. The participants may be an existing group.

- Determine who will keep (facilitate) the Circle. If you are planning to be the keeper, recruit someone who will support you in the responsibility of maintaining a safe space for respectful dialogue.

- Choose a time and place for the Talking Circle, keeping in mind the importance of warmth, hospitality, and access. Make sure the space allows for a sufficient number of chairs to be arranged in a circle with no furniture inside the circle.

- Extend invitations to possible participants with an explanation of the topic, the purpose of the Circle, and the nature of the process.

- Choose a talking piece that will have meaning to the group and will encourage respectful speaking and listening.

- Plan an opening ceremony to set the tone of the relationship space of the Circle (e.g. a reading, deep breathing, music). In planning this and the centerpiece below, make sure that you do not choose something that may be misunderstood or alienating to participants.

- Decide whether you wish to create a centerpiece for the Circle, such as a cloth with a candle or flowers, or other objects that have meaning related to the group or the topic.

- Decide whether you will have food at the Circle and make the necessary arrangements. (Food can be shared at the beginning or end of a Circle.)
- Draft questions that will help participants get acquainted and engage the topic of dialogue.
- Spend time reflecting or meditating on your intention and the importance of entering the Circle with openness and acceptance of others.

Stage 3: Convening

Having made the preparations, arrive early at the space. Make sure the physical set-up is appropriate. Set up the centerpiece if you have one planned. Take some time to breathe deeply and clear your mind of distractions. Follow these steps to convene the Circle:

- Greet participants as they arrive.
- When everyone is present and it is time to start, invite everyone to take a seat.
- Welcome everyone and thank them for coming.
- Conduct the opening ceremony.
- Share again the purpose of the Talking Circle and your intent.
- Introduce the talking piece and explain how it functions. Explain that the talking piece will be passed around the Circle, allowing everyone an opportunity to speak. Only the person holding the talking piece may speak. The only exception is that the keeper (facilitator) may speak without the talking piece if it is necessary for healthy functioning of the Circle. Emphasize that one can choose not to speak by passing the talking piece or holding it in silence.
- Develop guidelines. Describe the importance of the Circle as a place where people can speak their truth.

Pass the talking piece in order around the Circle and ask participants to identify promises they would like from the other participants for making the Circle a place where they can speak the truth.

Record the suggested guidelines on a flip chart or notepad. At the end of the round, read the list to the group. Ask the participants whether they can commit to those guidelines for their process. Pass the talking piece again for individual responses. If there is not consensus, seek modifications that everyone can accept.

- If there are time parameters for the Circle, explain those and ask participants to keep those in mind and to take responsibility for making sure that everyone has adequate opportunity to speak.

- Using the talking piece, initiate a round of introductions even if the participants already know one another. Pose a question for participants to answer in addition to saying who they are. This question is intended to help participants know more about each other before beginning the topic discussion.

  You might ask how the participants are connected to the organizer, or what life experience brought them to be interested in the topic, or what experience they have had with dialogue about difficult or controversial subjects. One purpose of this question is to help participants see commonalities even though they may have very different opinions on the topic. The keeper speaks first in this round and models the kind of sharing that is invited from the participants.

- Begin the dialogue about the chosen topic with a question inviting participants to share their thoughts and feelings about the issue. Pose the question for the group and pass the talking piece for responses. In this round it is usually good for the keeper to speak last.

- Pass the talking piece again for people to respond to what they have heard from others in the previous round.
- If there is time for additional passes of the talking piece, follow the major threads of dialogue that emerged in the earlier rounds.
- If people are interrupting, speaking without the talking piece, or are disrespectful in any way, suspend the dialogue about the issue and revisit the guidelines, asking participants if they can recommit to those guidelines or if any changes are needed.
- About 15 minutes before the ending time of the Circle, pass the talking piece again, asking participants for their feelings about the experience of the Circle or any closing comments they wish to make.
- Offer closing remarks that summarize the experience from your perspective, relate to the original intent, identify what you learned, and honor the achievement of the group in creating and maintaining respectful space. Thank everyone for participating and commiting to a respectful process.
- Conduct a closing ceremony that marks the end of the process, reminds people of their interconnectedness, and emphasizes positive potential (e.g. a reading, music, silent reflection).

Stage 4: Follow-up

Follow-up is critical for many kinds of Circles, but a Talking Circle does not generally require follow-up unless the group decides to continue its dialogue or take some further steps. As a keeper, you may wish to seek feedback from participants about what worked and what didn't in the process. Personal reflection on your role as a keeper and debriefing with your co-keeper or support person is always important following a Circle.

These steps are provided as a general guide. Circles are not rigid, but certain elements such as opening and closing ceremonies, use of the talking piece, and the creation of guidelines are essential. With minor modifications, the same steps are used for other types of Talking Circles. For example, the preparation stage for organizing a Check-In Circle or a Circle to reflect on a shared experience (e.g. in a classroom) is simpler, because the topic, participants, and place and time of the Circle are typically already determined.

9.
A Circle Story—
Finding Respect
Across Generations[14]

Two neighborhood organizations in Milwaukee became interested in restorative justice and began dialogue with David, a local prosecutor who has been very active in developing restorative practices in the city. They organized a short information session on Circles and remained in dialogue over a period of time, exploring ways to use a restorative approach to break the isolation experienced by many elderly and youth. That isolation breeds fear and mistrust, diminishing the quality of life, especially for seniors.

Barbara and Jeanne, the organizers, decided to hold a Talking Circle involving seniors and young people to assess the level of interest in using Peacemaking Circles in the future to address issues of isolation and personal safety for seniors and youth. They wanted to determine if there was enough interest in the process to justify investing in training for Peacemaking Circles.

In preparation they identified seniors to invite to the Circle. They chose seniors who had expressed both fear and a desire for a better relationship with youth. They worked in partnership with the local Boys and Girls Club and identified a leadership group of teens from the club program to invite to the Circle.

The invitations went to 22 seniors and 10 youth. The demographics of this neighborhood have changed dramatically over the years. The seniors were mostly white, the youth a mixture of African American, Hispanic, and white. The organizers asked David, the prosecutor, to keep the Circle because he is an experienced keeper. They chose the space (a room at the Boys and Girls Club) and time (3:30 to 5:00 p.m.) for the Circle and planned the food. They produced and distributed the invitation. They also planned the opening activity, which involved making masks for Mardi Gras.

In preparation, David as keeper chose the centerpiece and the talking piece for the Circle. In consultation with the organizers, David crafted the questions to use in the Circle.

The organizers arrived early to set up the food and the art materials for making masks. David set up the circle of chairs and the centerpiece, a wood carving of intertwined figures. He also took some quiet time to center himself and focus on deep breathing.

As people arrived for the Circle, they were greeted warmly and invited to make Mardi Gras masks with the art materials. Twelve of the invited seniors and 10 of the youth came to the Circle.

When the group convened in the circle of chairs, the organizers opened with remarks about Mardi Gras and the meaning of the masks. David introduced the talking piece, a beaded feather, and described the significance of the feather which had been given to him by colleagues after they attended a Circle training. David also described how the talking piece is used, emphasizing the importance of respectful speaking and listening.

Using the talking piece, David then invited participants to share their names and talk about how long they had lived in the neighborhood or had been coming to the Boys and Girls Club. One participant said that she had lived in the same house for 65 years, and she spoke at length about her history in the neighborhood.

For the second round of the talking piece, David invited people to share a story of something that makes them proud to live in this neighborhood or to be part of the Boys and Girls Club.

The third and final round of the talking piece offered participants the opportunity to share something they learned that day. One of the youth responded, "I learned that old people can be really cool." An older adult reflected that she learned it didn't matter what age you are or what race you are, you could still listen to one another.

At closing the participants stood and did a "penguin clap" by holding their arms slightly out from their sides so that their hands overlapped with the next person, and then clapped their hand against the hand of their neighbor on each side in the Circle. The "penguin clap" suggests connectedness without imposing intimacy and is very playful.

At the close of the Circle, two girls, who at times seemed not to be paying attention, went immediately up to some seniors and began talking with them. The girls expressed eagerness to do it again. The driver who transported the seniors home reported that they were thrilled with the experience and were very happy that they had participated. The group plans to do more work bringing seniors and youth together.

10.
Circles in Perspective

"This is terribly counter-cultural because we want quick fix-es. We are all starving for community. It's a wonderful place to go and say something and know you'll be heard. It gives us another way than just dividing people into us and them."
— Community Circle participant

Community-building impact

Storytelling is critical to the creation of community, connection, and collective action. And quantum physics tells us that it is not the content of matter which defines it but its relationships to other pieces of matter.

The process of weaving also provides a useful metaphor for building community. Relationships are like the threads in the fabric of a community, and the shared values of the culture and community create the framework, or loom, for weaving the relationships together.

As the spinning wheel is a tool for creating the threads, so is storytelling a tool for creating relationships. And as the shuttle weaves the threads into a fabric, the relationships woven together form community.

One of the most important contributions of Circles is the strengthened web of relationships among a group of people. It may be in a classroom, neighborhood, workplace, family, or faith group. As people sit together, talk about values, share personal stories, and work through disagreements in an atmosphere of respect and caring, they weave strong cords of connection among themselves. Those connections increase the community's capacity to take care of all its members and to find solutions when problems arise.

Circles offer the opportunity for members of a community to converse about what they expect from each other and what they are willing to commit to in terms of standards of behavior. In Circles they can build those standards of behavior from shared values and an understanding of how their choices impact others.

How is a Circle different from other similar processes?

There are a variety of processes that look similar to Peacemaking Circles and share key characteristics. Because of the similarities, some people assume that Circles are the same as these processes. Circles differ from these processes in significant ways that affect relationships and outcomes.

Circles and groups

Staff in a juvenile correctional facility, upon learning about Peacemaking Circles, suggested that the groups they do with youth are the same as Circles. In a subsequent

"What do you do here?" a woman asked, noting that the atmosphere around the building had changed. "There were always lots of kids hanging around, making a lot of noise and they never helped open the door when my arms were loaded. Now it's quieter and when they are around, they run to open the door for me."

The woman she was addressing had led several Circles with neighborhood kids and it had apparently changed the climate of the neighborhood.[15]

training with youth in that facility, the youth were asked if the Circle was the same as their groups. They answered with an emphatic "NO." The youth identified power considerations as a key difference.

In their groups, the facilitator is judging and evaluating their behavior and level of participation. The facilitator has specific expectations about what the youth should say or not say. Under those circumstances, the youth frequently do not feel safe to speak their truth. If one person in a group has power over others and can use what happens in the group in an evaluative process without consensus of the group, then it is not a Peacemaking Circle. The youth were very aware that in group they are not all equal, which is a core prerequisite of Circles.

Circles and therapy

In a Peacemaking Circle, clinical or professional expertise is not the primary resource for gaining insight or for understanding issues. Storytelling by the participants, based on their personal narratives, and self reflection are the main sources of insight.

Additionally, unlike in most therapy, the keeper in a Circle is a participant and may share life experiences that are relevant to the Circle dialogue. A therapist may be a participant in a Circle and share clinical expertise as part of the information the Circle considers, but the therapist would not be responsible for managing all the dynamics of the Circle as they typically might in a therapy role. The Circle facilitator does not direct or manage the work of the group. In a Circle, participants are not only responsible for their own behavior but they share responsibility for the quality of the space of the group as a whole.

Circles and classroom meetings

Many classroom management books and social skills curricula, particularly on the elementary and middle-school level, encourage using the class meeting. The class meeting is a time when students learn and practice social skills such as giving and receiving compliments, listening, empathy, problem-solving, conflict resolution, anger management and identification, and expression of feelings.

These skills are taught through games or activities, often while the students are sitting in a circle. However, key Circle elements may be missing from these activities, such as the use of the talking piece, permission to pass, and the clear expectation that the piece will go around the circle in order.

Challenges

The Circle Process is based on a simple notion: Because we all want to be in good relationships with others, when we create a space that is respectful and reflective, people can find their way through anger, pain, and fear to find common ground and take care of one another. Though the concept is simple, the practice is not.

In many ways our culture encourages separation, demonization of those who disagree, competition, hierarchy, and reliance on experts to solve problems. These tendencies in our collective life create a powerful momentum in a direction opposite that of Circles.

Circles are raising very difficult questions of meaning and personal commitment in the context of community life: What does spirituality mean in a public process? How do we honor one another's spiritual expression? What symbols are meaningful in a diverse culture? How do we invest meaning in symbols and keep that meaning fresh and vibrant? What is the responsibility of the individual to the larger whole? What are our fundamental assumptions about human nature? What does "speaking from the heart" require of us? Can we keep our hearts open when something hurts us? Can we truly live these values?

Common struggles are apparent in various Circle groups. It is very challenging to shift from giving advice and providing answers to sharing personal stories and raising genuine questions (ones to which you do not already have the answer). Most Circles struggle to find that tone which recognizes that we are all inseparable parts of a whole.

Circles raise difficult questions of meaning and personal commitment in the context of community life.

Many Circles are also struggling with the relationship between the lay members and system professionals who sit in Circle. The new roles for professionals are not clear. We tell them to leave their title at the door, but it is not that simple in practice. Professionals have information that is useful to the Circle and they have responsibilities that do not end when they are in Circle.

The interface between the Circle Process and social institutions is very sensitive. The Circle seeks truth and aims to create a space in which participants feel safe to speak their truth knowing that, though they must be accountable for their actions, they will not be disrespected or deliberately harmed. If information revealed in Circle triggers an adversarial process, the resulting actions may betray the Circle's commitment to honor the dignity and voice of every person.

Mandatory reporting creates a dilemma—not because the information should be kept secret but because the information may be revealed in an atmosphere that promises respectful treatment even for those who have made mistakes. Yet the Circle cannot guarantee respectful, non-harming treatment once the information is reported to an adversarial system.

Issues of confidentiality are very thorny in practice. It is critical to elicit truth in order to resolve problems, but there is enormous responsibility to make sure that truth-telling does not put people in jeopardy of harm to their essential being.

Because decisions in Circle are made by consensus, pressure may be put on someone who does not agree to simply go along. This pressure may be felt even if nothing is said. People who have not experienced power or voice in their lives may assume that they had better go along with the rest of the group whether they agree or not. It takes consistent and repeated effort to convey to all participants that their truth and perspective is welcomed, even when it means that the process is prolonged because consensus has not been reached.

For advocates of Circles, it is a challenge to refrain from making judgments about people who erect barriers to Circles or who work against the vision of Circles. The Circle asks us to remain open to everyone and to honor the inherent dignity of everyone—even when that person may not be honoring the inherent dignity of someone else or the values we hold dear in Circle. The power of the vision sometimes evokes a passion that blunts the ability to deeply hear voices that disagree.

Even when Circles do not reach the full flow of human heart and spirit, they are usually powerful. Several weeks after a widely criticized court case, the judge reflected, "There were faults. This didn't work perfectly. But as I sit here and think about it, this worked as well as any case in court."

11.
A Circle Story—
Finding Connection Within Family[16]

For the holidays this year, my nieces and nephews, who normally exchange gifts, decided instead to donate their gift money to a charity—a rather huge step for a bunch of teenagers and college kids. The kids ended up donating over a hundred dollars to an organization for battered women and children. They had no expectations of gifts at our extended family gathering. Just being together was what mattered most to them.

We gathered for our extended family holiday celebration, as usual, on New Year's Eve: four of my brothers, two sisters, and all of our kids for a grand total of 22 individuals. After presenting my mother—"Grandma"—with a new table-top keyboard, a few gifts managed to find their way into the room. Boxes of candy were presented by some, baskets or books from another. Tape measures for all of the guys from the carpenter. I, on the other hand, thought we had agreed to no gifts and stuck to it. I sat there, watching those who just couldn't let gifts "go," and at that moment decided to give them a gift of my own.

Grandma finished her rendition of "The Entertainer" on her new keyboard, and I asked the family to be seated so I could present my gift to them. We were already in somewhat of a circle, so the space was set. I shared with my brothers, sisters, mother, and all of our kids what the staff at Minnesota Correctional Facility Initiative in Moose Lake have been attempting with the Conflict Resolution Initiative: to improve communication, build relationship, and change culture.

I explained a Circle and its intent, and asked permission to share this "gift of communication" with them. Rather timidly my family agreed. I chose for a talking piece a basket that I had just received and suggested that when they see that basket at the cabin, they think of all of the things we shared in this Circle during the holidays.

My question to my family was, "What in the past year has touched you?" and "What do you look forward to in the next year?" The honesty of emotions presented and the depth to which they went surprised even me. A death in the family, loneliness at college, elation over a scholarship, the loss of a job, service in Iraq, thankfulness for a promotion, and many more memories from the past year were shared. Hopes for the future included looking forward to being with family, vacations, being with cousins, and having loved ones home from service.

I reluctantly ended the Circle after three passes of the talking piece, but further discussion of the content went on throughout the evening. Family members tearfully thanked me for this "gift" and look forward to doing it again.

Keeping in touch—communicating—through good and bad is vital to all of us, no matter where we work, but it is especially vital to family.

12.
Conclusion

"Circles take the hard things and bring out the beauty."
— Circle participant

I offer this book with the recognition that it describes my own understanding of Circles. Although many wonderful mentors have shaped my understanding, any particular point of view is limited because it is the view of one point on the rim of the Circle. I can only know my truth. I cannot know the truth for others.

I am deeply grateful for the teachers who brought Circles into my life and for the hundreds and hundreds of people who have shared with me in Circle profound stories of personal struggles. In Circle, through the stories of others and in sharing my own story, I have learned more about who I am and have found my place in community. And in the marvelously paradoxical nature of Circles, while finding my place I also found greater humility—a greater awareness of the limitations of my place.

Peacemaking Circles provide a way to bring people together to hold difficult conversations and to work through conflict or differences. The Circle Process is a way of getting the most complete picture people can of themselves, of one another, and of the issues at hand to enable them to move together in a good way. Circles are based on an assumption of positive potential: that something good can always come out of whatever situation we are in. Circles also assume that no one of us has the whole picture, that it is only by sharing all of our perspectives that we can come closer to a complete picture. Sharing individual perspectives and wisdom creates a collective wisdom much greater than the sum of the parts.

I believe that the Circle is a pathway for bringing together ancient wisdom of communal life with modern wisdom about individual gifts and the value of dissent and difference. In a Circle we honor each individual *and* we honor the collective. In a Circle we reach deep within ourselves *and* we reach outward to connect to the community of the Circle.

Modern Western societies struggle with a lack of connection and with a failure to recognize their interrelatedness. On the other hand, many highly communal societies struggle to make space for different voices and perspectives. In our wonderfully complex, multi-cultural society, those two worldviews are living side by side and have the opportunity to learn directly from each other. The Circle is a crucible for that learning. In the Circle we can find a healthy balance between individual and group needs.

I believe that the Circle is also a pathway for healing past harms as a society. Shame and the fear of losing love or respect are enormous barriers to facing harm we have caused.

When whole societies or groups of people need to acknowledge harm, it is even more difficult. In a Circle we acknowledge our mistakes *and* we hold ourselves and each other in compassion. We are never alone in a Circle. That compassion and the connection we feel to others create an environment in which we can face the painful reality of our impact on others. From acknowledgment can begin the healing process for ourselves and for those who were harmed.

Conclusion

We have only begun to scratch the surface of ways in which the Circle Process can change the content and meaning of our lives. We are limited only by our imaginations, our willingness to be in respectful and loving relationship with every part of creation, and our ability to allow the pattern of the Circle to emerge without trying to manage or control it.

My understanding of Circles continues to evolve. I share my thoughts about Circles not as absolutes, but as part of a continuing dialogue and journey of learning. And I am grateful for the interst and gifts others bring to this exploration of our human capacity for connection and reflection.

The Same

> This is a time when
> Doing
> is split off from
> Knowing,
> and Being
> is
> hardly at all.
>
> But here and there
> on this side of the horizon,
> people meet in sacred circles
> to form communities
> and speak their hearts
> that seek the same.[18]
> — Meir Carasso

Appendix 1
The Circle Process in Schools

Cynthia Zwicky, M.Ed., Minneapolis Public Schools

The Circle Process and schools are a natural fit. There are many ways that the Circle has been incorporated into the fabric of the Minneapolis Public Schools.

Circles for conflict resolution

Schools are a place where teaching and learning occur naturally. Sometimes this occurs through lessons planned and taught by a teacher, but it can also occur at the hands or words of a peer. Schools are a place where conflict is a daily occurrence as well. Therefore, they provide the perfect setting for teaching and learning about conflict resolution, and the Circle becomes an essential tool for the lesson.

In one third-grade classroom, a teacher had been using the Circle for a variety of purposes. Having become acquainted with the Circle Process, several girls in this class who were struggling with following school rules and staying out of trouble got together on their own during recess to hold a daily Circle. The purpose of the Circle was to support one another to stay on the right path. They set goals for themselves and used this Circle time to check in on their personal progress.

The Circle is, by design, inclusive and equal. Because of this, it can become a place where anyone participating helps find the solution. One example is from a multi-aged classroom of six- to nine-year-olds. On the playground, one boy had knocked down a girl classmate and lain on top of her. This left her shaken, and friends on the playground came to comfort her.

That afternoon, during the classroom Circle, she acknowledged her friends for helping her when she was scared. Curious, another student asked why she was scared, and she explained what happened. The teacher confessed to the group that she did not know how to respond. Then she opened it up for them to respond. As the Circle proceeded, the students began to find the solution.

Finally one student confronted the boy, "Why did you do that to her?" He responded, in a subdued voice, "Because I like her." The response came from the students, "Then why don't you do something so she likes you back?"

The teacher knows that she would not have been able to come up with that solution. It was through the power of the Circle, and collective responsibility, that the issue was resolved.

Community-building Circles

At the beginning of the school year, every teacher gets her/his class list and anticipates the arrival of the new students. As the year begins, Circles are often used to build community. Developing a healthy classroom community creates a foundation for conflict resolution.

We *learn* to be in community—it doesn't always happen by virtue of being in the same place at the same time. Students who have benefited from the use of a daily Circle in their classroom noticed a difference from previous years. "I know everyone's name in my class this year, and I didn't last year," said a sixth grader. The Circle provides everyone the opportunity to speak and to be heard. In this way, we can be assured that no one gets left out.

Perhaps equally important and often overlooked is the importance of building community among adults. Relational trust between teachers is an important factor in student achievement. In one school, it was the teachers who first sat in Circle together at the beginning of the school year and then used it in their classrooms with their students.

They noted the positive effects immediately in the same way their students did. One commented, "We've been working together for four years, and I never knew your son went to the same school as my daughter!" Learning first-hand how beneficial the Circle could be to building community has provided a strong impetus for teachers to begin practicing it in their own classrooms.

Circles as a part of the curriculum

Teachers have also used the Circle as a place to teach a lesson. In a seventh-grade social studies class, the teacher had the students discuss their reactions to the movie *Roots* while they sat in Circle as an alternative to filling out a worksheet. The interactive forum provided the students the opportunity to go deeper into the meaning and their personal feelings around this difficult and complex movie.

Because Circles are a place where the person as an individual is valued, it becomes a safe place to learn and discuss opinions expressed from the heart. It benefits the teachers because they are able to hear every student's voice, something that is not always possible during a whole-class discussion.

The Circle can also be used to strengthen existing curricula. Numerous social skills and anti-bullying curricula encourage students to speak up when they are being teased. Teaching these strategies in the Circle can also provide students with an ideal forum for speaking out. With an established protocol for using the Circle in one's classroom, students will be more likely to try some of the new strategies and coping skills identified in many of these curricula.

The Circle can also be a place where students learn from each other's challenges and successes. A middle school student who had used the Circle reports, "I like [using the Circle] because if someone is having the same problem as you are, you can listen and hear how they solved it."

Conclusion

The uses for Circles in school settings are infinite and are by no means limited to the ones described here. In preparing future generations for this world, the Circle becomes an essential tool for imparting knowledge, providing a forum for reflective dialogue, and encouraging the use of creative and peaceful solutions to conflict. The possibilities are endless.

Endnotes

1 From "Soul Food," *The Well* no. 7 (March 2002). This is hte online newsletter of the Church Council on Justice and Corrections, Ottawa, Canada. See www.ccjc.ca.

2 For more information about Circles, see Pranis, Stuart, and Wedge.

3 For an overview of restorative justice, see Howard Zehr.

4 From a report on In-School Behavior Intervention Grants. See www.education.state.mn.us.

5 Matt Johnson wrote this description of a Circle Process he facilitated with Paula Schaefer while working for AMICUS, a non-profit organization working wiht prison inmates and parolees in Minneapolis, MN.

6 See Pranis, Stuart, and Wedge.

7 (San Francisco: Berrett-Koehler Publishers, 1992.)

8 Ibid., pp. 6, 8-9

9 Ibid., pp. 9-10

10 From a Minnesota Department of Education report on In-School Behavior Intervention Grants. See www.education.state.mn.us.

11 The how-to's of monitoring versus enforcing are subtle skills that require specific training and more explanation than can be provided in a book of this length.

12 Story provided by the author.

13 Ibid.

14 Ibid.

15 Ibid.

16 By Cindy Zetah, "The Gift of Circle," *CRI Newsletter* (February 2004), p. 3.

Suggested Reading

Baldwin, Christina. *Calling the Circle: The First and Future Culture* (Newberg, OR: Swan-Raven, 1994; reprint, New York: Bantam Doubleday Dell, 1998).

Bolen, Jean Shinoda. *The Millionth Circle—How to Change Ourselves and the World: The Essential Guide to Women's Circles* (Berkeley: Conari Press, 1999).

Bopp, Judie, et al., *The Sacred Tree: Reflections on Native American Spirituality* (Lethbridge, Alberta: Four Worlds International Institute,1984).

Boyes-Watson, Carolyn. *Holding the Space: The Journey of Circles at Roca* (Boston: The Center for Restorative Justice at Suffolk University, 2002).

Engel, Beverly. *Women Circling the Earth: A Guide to Fostering Community, Healing, and Empowerment* (Deerfield Beach, FL: Health Communications, 2000).

Garfield, Charles, Cindy Spring, and Sedonia Cahill. *Wisdom Circles: A Guide to Self-Discovery and Community Building in Small Groups* (New York: Hyperion, 1998).

Pranis, Kay, Barry Stuart, and Mark Wedge. *Peacemaking Circles: From Crime to Community* (St. Paul: Living Justice Press, 2003). See www.livingjusticepress.org.

Ross, Rupert. *Returning to the Teachings: Exploring Aboriginal Justice* (Toronto: Penguin Books Canada, 1996).

Wheatley, Margaret J. *Leadership and the New Science* (San Francisco: Berrett-Koehler Publishers, 1992).

Zehr, Howard. *The Little Book of Restorative Justice* (Intercourse, PA: Good Books, 2002).

Zimmerman, Jack, with Virginia Coyle. *The Way of Council* (Las Vegas: Bramble Books, 1996).

About the Author

Kay Pranis is a trainer and writer on Peacemaking Circles and restorative justice. She served as the Restorative Justice Planner for the Minnesota Department of Corrections from 1994 to 2003.

Since 1998, Kay has conducted Circle trainings in a diverse range of communities—from schools to prisons to workplaces to churches, and from rural towns in Minnesota to Chicago's South Side to Montgomery, Alabama. She has written numerous articles on restorative justice and co-wrote *Peacemaking Circles: From Crime to Community.*

Kay's intention in her work is to create spaces in which people can be in more loving connection with each other. Kay's experience as a parent and a community activist form the foundation of her vision for peacemaking and community-building.

She is available for Circle trainings and can be reached at kaypranis@msn.com or at 651/698-9181.

METHOD OF PAYMENT

❐ Check or Money Order
  *(payable to **Good Books** in U.S. funds)*

❐ Please charge my:
    ❐ MasterCard   ❐ Visa
    ❐ Discover   ❐ American Express

\# _____

exp. date _____

Signature _____

Name _____

Address _____

City _____

State _____

Zip _____

Phone _____

Email _____

SHIP TO: (if different)

Name _____

Address _____

City _____

State _____

Zip _____

Mail order to: **Good Books**
P.O. Box 419 • Intercourse, PA 17534-0419
Call toll-free: 800/762-7171
Fax toll-free: 888/768-3433
Prices subject to change.

Group Discounts for

The Little Book of
Circle Processes
ORDER FORM

If you would like to order multiple copies of *The Little Book of Circle Processes* by Kay Pranis for groups you know or are a part of, use this form. (Discounts apply only for more than one copy.)
Photocopy this page as often as you like.

The following discounts apply:

1 copy	$4.95
2-5 copies	$4.45 each (a 10% discount)
6-10 copies	$4.20 each (a 15% discount)
11-20 copies	$3.96 each (a 20% discount)
21-99 copies	$3.45 each (a 30% discount)
100 or more	$2.97 each (a 40% discount)

Free shipping for U.S. orders of 100 or more!
Prices subject to change.

Quantity   *Price*   *Total*

_____ copies of **Circle Processes**   @ _____   _____

Shipping & Handling
(U.S. orders only: add 10%; $3.95 minimum) _____
For international orders, please call 800/762-7171, ext. 221

PA residents add 6% sales tax _____

TOTAL _____
